a bouquet of

Tender Promises

to give you hope

Tyndale House Publishers, Inc.

CAROL STREAM, ILLINOIS

Because of [God's] glory and excellence,
he has given us great and precious
promises. These are the promises that
enable you to share his divine nature
and escape the world's corruption caused
by human desires.

2 PETER 1:4

All the LORD's promises prove true. He is a shield for all who look to him for protection.

2 SAMUEL 22:31

Deep in your hearts you know that every promise of the LORD your God has come true. Not a single one has failed!

JOSHUA 23:14

I publicly proclaim bold promises. I do not
whisper obscurities in some dark corner.
I would not have told the people of Israel
to seek me if I could not be found. I, the
LORD, speak only what is true and declare
only what is right.

ISAIAH 45:19

God is not a man, so he does not lie. He is not human, so he does not change his mind. Has he ever spoken and failed to act? Has he ever promised and not carried it through?

NUMBERS 23:19

The LORD has declared
today that you are
his people, his own
special treasure,
just as he promised.

DEUTERONOMY 26:18

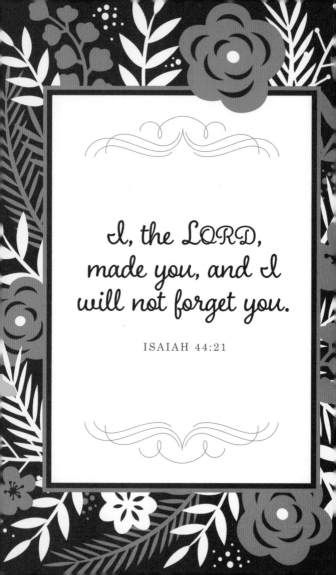

I, the LORD,
made you, and I
will not forget you.

ISAIAH 44:21

I will be your God throughout your lifetime—until your hair is white with age. I made you, and I will care for you. I will carry you along and save you. . . . I have said what I would do, and I will do it.

ISAIAH 46:4, 11

You are all children of God through faith in Christ Jesus. And all who have been united with Christ in baptism have put on Christ, like putting on new clothes. . . . And now that you belong to Christ, you are the true children of Abraham. You are his heirs, and God's promise to Abraham belongs to you.

GALATIANS 3:26-27, 29

You will show us
your faithfulness and
unfailing love as
you promised to our
ancestors Abraham
and Jacob long ago.

MICAH 7:20

With your unfailing love you lead the people you have redeemed. In your might, you guide them to your sacred home.

EXODUS 15:13

Stand here quietly before the LORD as I
remind you of all the great things the
LORD has done for you and your ancestors.
. . . The LORD will not abandon his people,
because that would dishonor his great name.
For it has pleased the LORD to make you
his very own people.

1 SAMUEL 12:7, 22

The rain and snow come down from the
heavens and stay on the ground to water
the earth. They cause the grain to grow,
producing seed for the farmer and bread for
the hungry. It is the same with my word.
I send it out, and it always produces fruit.
It will accomplish all I want it to, and it
will prosper everywhere I send it.

ISAIAH 55:10-11

The Scriptures give us hope
and encouragement as we
*wait patiently
for God's promises
to be fulfilled.*

ROMANS 15:4

Your word is a lamp
to guide my feet and
a light for my path.

PSALM 119:105

[Moses said,] "Commit yourselves wholeheartedly to these words of mine. . . . Teach them to your children. Talk about them when you are at home and when you are on the road, when you are going to bed and when you are getting up . . . so that as long as the sky remains above the earth, you and your children may flourish."

DEUTERONOMY 11:18-19, 21

Not one word
has failed of all
the wonderful
promises [God]
gave through his
servant Moses.

1 KINGS 8:56

His way is perfect; the word of the LORD is proven; He is a shield to all who trust in Him.

PSALM 18:30, NKJV

The LORD God is our sun and our shield.
He gives us grace and glory. The LORD will
withhold no good thing from those who do
what is right. O LORD of Heaven's Armies,
what joy for those who trust in you.

PSALM 84:11-12

Let the godly sing for joy to the LORD;

it is fitting for the pure to praise him.

. . . The LORD's plans stand firm forever;

his intentions can never be shaken. . . .

The LORD watches over those who fear him,

those who rely on his unfailing love.

PSALM 33:1, 11, 18

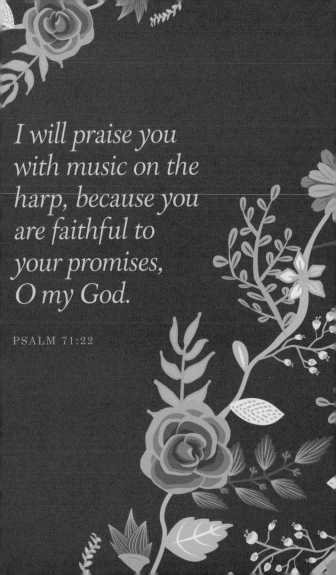

*I will praise you
with music on the
harp, because you
are faithful to
your promises,
O my God.*

PSALM 71:22

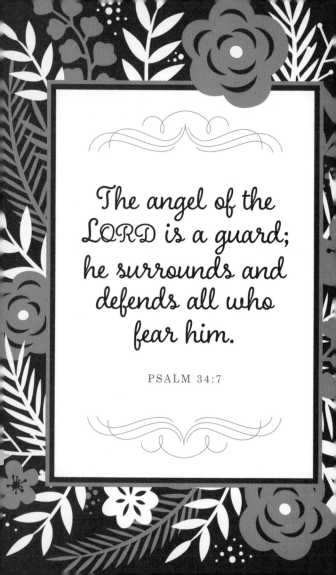

The angel of the
LORD is a guard;
he surrounds and
defends all who
fear him.

PSALM 34:7

Praise the LORD, who is my rock. He trains my hands for war and gives my fingers skill for battle. He is my loving ally and my fortress, my tower of safety, my rescuer. He is my shield, and I take refuge in him. He makes the nations submit to me.

PSALM 144:1-2

Do not dread the disease that stalks in darkness, nor the disaster that strikes at midday. . . . The LORD says, "I will rescue those who love me. I will protect those who trust in my name. When they call on me, I will answer; I will be with them in trouble. I will rescue and honor them. I will reward them with a long life and give them my salvation."

PSALM 91:6, 14-16

Because you trusted me . . . I will rescue you and keep you safe. I, the LORD, have spoken!

JEREMIAH 39:18

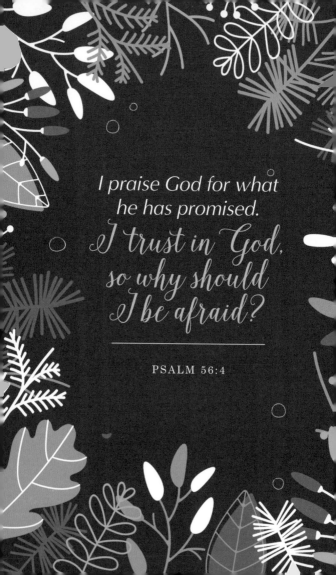

I praise God for what he has promised. ℐ *trust in God, so why should ℐ be afraid?*

PSALM 56:4

You keep track of all my sorrows. You have
collected all my tears in your bottle. You
have recorded each one in your book. My
enemies will retreat when I call to you
for help. This I know: God is on my side!
. . . What can mere mortals do to me? I will
fulfill my vows to you, O God, and will offer
a sacrifice of thanks for your help.

PSALM 56:8-9, 11-12

Have mercy on me, O God, have mercy! I look
to you for protection. I will hide beneath
the shadow of your wings until the danger
passes by. I cry out to God Most High, to
God who will fulfill his purpose for me.
He will send help from heaven to rescue
me, disgracing those who hound me. My
God will send forth his unfailing love
and faithfulness.

PSALM 57:1-3

I will save you from the
hands of the wicked

*and deliver you
from the grasp of
the cruel.*

JEREMIAH 15:21, NIV

You have done
many good things
for me, LORD, just
as you promised.

PSALM 119:65

I hold you by your right hand—I, the LORD
your God. And I say to you, "Don't be afraid.
I am here to help you. . . . I am the LORD,
your Redeemer. I am the Holy One of Israel."

ISAIAH 41:13-14

The LORD will
fight for you;
you need only
to be still.

EXODUS 14:14, NIV

Though the mountains
be shaken and the hills
be removed, yet my
unfailing love for you
will not be shaken.

ISAIAH 54:10, NIV

Sing praises to the LORD, O you his saints, and give thanks to his holy name. For his anger is but for a moment, and his favor is for a lifetime. Weeping may tarry for the night, but joy comes with the morning.

PSALM 30:4-5, ESV

This I call to mind, and therefore I have hope: The steadfast love of the LORD never ceases; his mercies never come to an end; they are new every morning; great is your faithfulness. "The LORD is my portion," says my soul, "therefore I will hope in him."

LAMENTATIONS 3:21-24, ESV

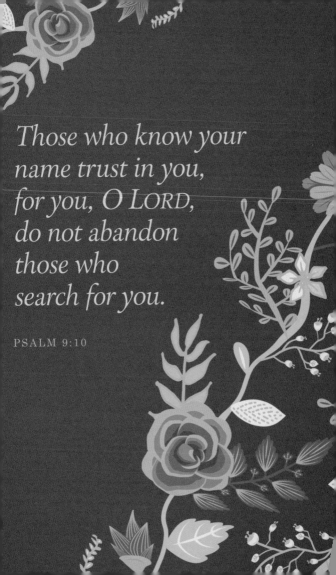

Those who know your
name trust in you,
for you, O LORD,
do not abandon
those who
search for you.

PSALM 9:10

I will not break my covenant; I will not take back a single word I said.

PSALM 89:34

I will never again curse the ground because
of the human race, even though everything
they think or imagine is bent toward evil
from childhood. I will never again destroy
all living things. As long as the earth
remains, there will be planting and harvest,
cold and heat, summer and winter, day
and night.

GENESIS 8:21-22

This I declare about the LORD: He alone is my refuge, my place of safety; he is my God, and I trust him. For he will rescue you from every trap and protect you from deadly disease. He will cover you with his feathers. He will shelter you with his wings. His faithful promises are your armor and protection.

PSALM 91:2-4

The LORD is
a shelter for the
oppressed, a refuge
in times of trouble.

PSALM 9:9

The kingdom of
the world has become
the kingdom
of our Lord and
of his Messiah,
and he will reign
for ever and ever.

REVELATION 11:15, NIV

The peoples hear and tremble. . . . The power of your arm makes them lifeless as stone until your people pass by, O LORD, until the people you purchased pass by. You will bring them in and plant them on your own mountain—the place, O LORD, reserved for your own dwelling, the sanctuary, O Lord, that your hands have established. The LORD will reign forever and ever!

EXODUS 15:14, 16-18

"Yes," says the LORD, "I will do mighty miracles for you, like those I did when I rescued you from slavery in Egypt." All the nations of the world will stand amazed at what the LORD will do for you. . . . . Where is another God like you, who pardons the guilt of the remnant, overlooking the sins of his special people?

MICAH 7:15-16, 18

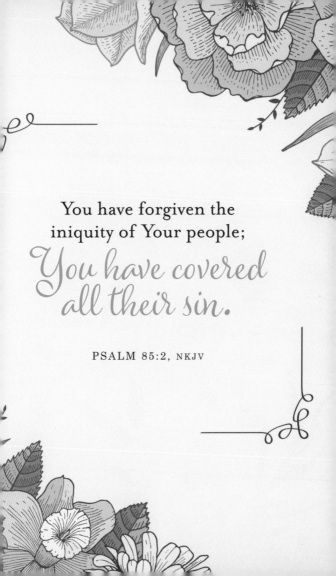

You have forgiven the
iniquity of Your people;
*You have covered
all their sin.*

PSALM 85:2, NKJV

You will have
compassion on us.
You will trample
our sins under your
feet and throw
them into the depths
of the ocean!

MICAH 7:19

See, the Sovereign LORD comes with power,
and he rules with a mighty arm. See, his
reward is with him, and his recompense
accompanies him. He tends his flock like a
shepherd: He gathers the lambs in his arms
and carries them close to his heart; he
gently leads those that have young.

ISAIAH 40:10-11, NIV

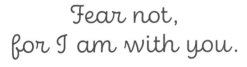

Fear not,
for I am with you.

ISAIAH 43:5, ESV

Humble yourselves in the sight of the Lord, and He will lift you up.

JAMES 4:10, NKJV

Show me the right path, O LORD; point out the road for me to follow. Lead me by your truth and teach me, for you are the God who saves me. . . . The LORD is good and does what is right; he shows the proper path to those who go astray. He leads the humble in doing right, teaching them his way.

PSALM 25:4-5, 8-9

I will pour out my Spirit on all people. Your
sons and daughters will prophesy, your old
men will dream dreams, your young men will
see visions. . . . I will show wonders in the
heavens and on the earth. . . . And everyone
who calls on the name of the LORD will
be saved.

JOEL 2:28, 30, 32, NIV

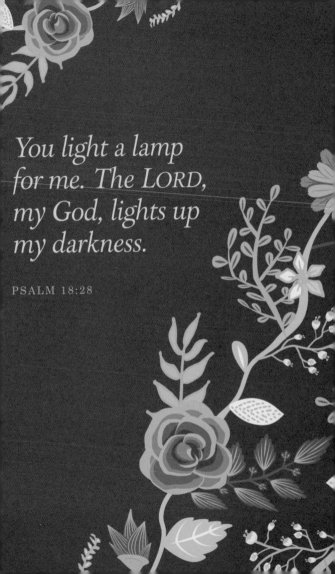

You light a lamp
for me. The LORD,
my God, lights up
my darkness.

PSALM 18:28

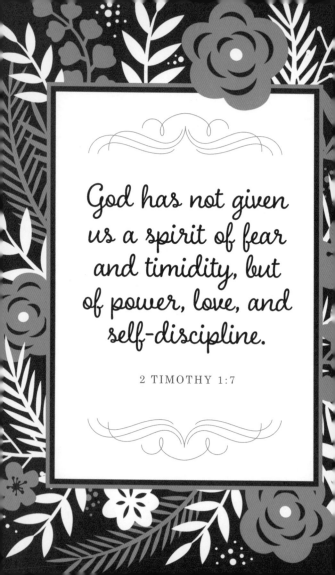

God has not given us a spirit of fear and timidity, but of power, love, and self-discipline.

2 TIMOTHY 1:7

Be strong and of good courage, do not fear nor be afraid . . . for the LORD your God, He is the One who goes with you. He will not leave you nor forsake you. . . . The LORD, He is the One who goes before you. He will be with you, He will not leave you nor forsake you; do not fear nor be dismayed.

DEUTERONOMY 31:6, 8, NKJV

"No weapon forged against you will prevail, and you will refute every tongue that accuses you. This is the heritage of the servants of the LORD, and this is their vindication from me," declares the LORD.

ISAIAH 54:17, NIV

Submit yourselves
therefore to God.
Resist the devil, and
he will flee from you.

JAMES 4:7, KJV

The LORD . . .
heals the
brokenhearted
and bandages
their wounds.

PSALM 147:2-3

The Spirit of the Sovereign LORD is upon me,
for the LORD has anointed me to bring good
news to the poor. He has sent me to comfort
the brokenhearted and to proclaim that
captives will be released and prisoners will
be freed.

ISAIAH 61:1

I tell you the truth, those who listen to my message and believe in God who sent me have eternal life. They will never be condemned for their sins, but they have already passed from death into life. And I assure you that the time is coming, indeed it's here now, when the dead will hear my voice—the voice of the Son of God. And those who listen will live.

JOHN 5:24-25

There is therefore
now no condemnation
*for those who are
in Christ Jesus.*

ROMANS 8:1, ESV

The love of the LORD
remains forever
*with those who fear
him. His salvation
extends to the
children's children.*

PSALM 103:17

Not a single sparrow can fall to the ground
without your Father knowing it. And the
very hairs on your head are all numbered.
So don't be afraid; you are more valuable
to God than a whole flock of sparrows.

MATTHEW 10:29-31

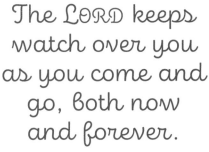

The LORD keeps
watch over you
as you come and
go, both now
and forever.

PSALM 121:8

Fear of the LORD is the foundation of true wisdom. All who obey his commandments will grow in wisdom.

PSALM 111:10

You are my friends if you do what I command. I no longer call you servants, because a servant does not know his master's business. Instead, I have called you friends, for everything that I learned from my Father I have made known to you.

JOHN 15:14-15, NIV

Jesus said, "Come to me, all of you who are weary and carry heavy burdens, and I will give you rest. Take my yoke upon you. Let me teach you, because I am humble and gentle at heart, and you will find rest for your souls. For my yoke is easy to bear, and the burden I give you is light."

MATTHEW 11:28-30

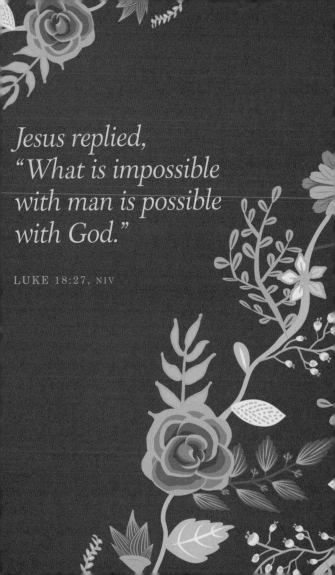

Jesus replied,
"What is impossible
with man is possible
with God."

LUKE 18:27, NIV

With God's
help we will do
mighty things.

PSALM 60:12

"You don't have enough faith," Jesus told them. "I tell you the truth, if you had faith even as small as a mustard seed, you could say to this mountain, 'Move from here to there,' and it would move. Nothing would be impossible."

MATTHEW 17:20

You fathers—if your children ask for a fish, do you give them a snake instead? Or if they ask for an egg, do you give them a scorpion? Of course not! So if you sinful people know how to give good gifts to your children, how much more will your heavenly Father give the Holy Spirit to those who ask him.

LUKE 11:11-13

Whatever you ask in
My name, that
I will do, that the
Father may be
glorified in the Son.

JOHN 14:13, NKJV

[Jesus] said . . .
"I will send the
Holy Spirit,
just as my
Father promised."

LUKE 24:44, 49

You shall receive power when the Holy Spirit has come upon you; and you shall be witnesses to Me in Jerusalem, and in all Judea and Samaria, and to the end of the earth.

ACTS 1:8, NKJV

When He, the Spirit of truth, has come, He will guide you into all truth; for He will not speak on His own authority, but whatever He hears He will speak; and He will tell you things to come.

JOHN 16:13, NKJV

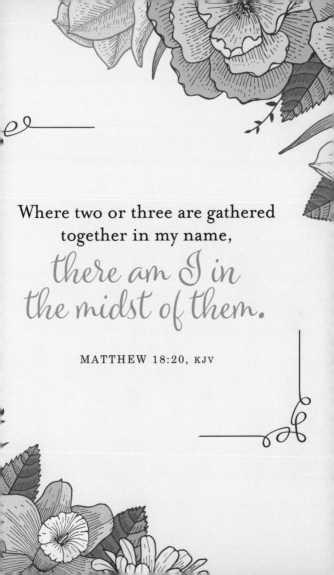

Where two or three are gathered
together in my name,

*there am I in
the midst of them.*

MATTHEW 18:20, KJV

The grass withers,
the flower fades,
but the word
of our God will
stand forever.

ISAIAH 40:8, ESV

Jesus replied, . . . "My sheep listen to my voice; I know them, and they follow me. I give them eternal life, and they will never perish. No one can snatch them away from me, for my Father has given them to me, and he is more powerful than anyone else. No one can snatch them from the Father's hand. The Father and I are one."

JOHN 10:25, 27-30

I shall not die,
but live, and
declare the
works of
the LORD.

 PSALM 118:17, NKJV

LORD, you will
grant us peace;
all we have accomplished
is really from you.

ISAIAH 26:12

Remain in me, and I will remain in you. For a branch cannot produce fruit if it is severed from the vine, and you cannot be fruitful unless you remain in me. Yes, I am the vine; you are the branches. Those who remain in me, and I in them, will produce much fruit. For apart from me you can do nothing.

JOHN 15:4-5

Whoever wants to be my disciple must deny themselves and take up their cross and follow me. For whoever wants to save their life will lose it, but whoever loses their life for me and for the gospel will save it.

MARK 8:34-35, NIV

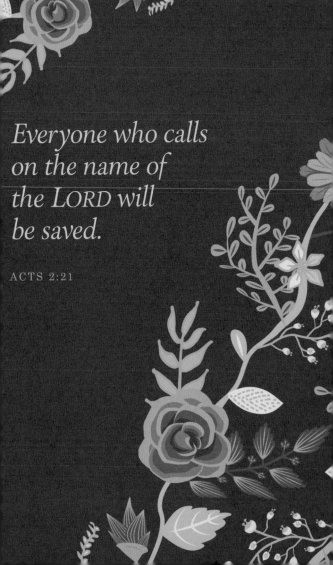

Everyone who calls
on the name of
the LORD will
be saved.

ACTS 2:21

If anyone is in Christ, the new creation has come: The old has gone, the new is here!

2 CORINTHIANS 5:17, NIV

[God] has reconciled you to himself through the death of Christ in his physical body. As a result, he has brought you into his own presence, and you are holy and blameless as you stand before him without a single fault.

COLOSSIANS 1:22

God has given both his promise and his oath. These two things are unchangeable because it is impossible for God to lie. Therefore, we who have fled to him for refuge can have great confidence as we hold to the hope that lies before us. This hope is a strong and trustworthy anchor for our souls. It leads us through the curtain into God's inner sanctuary.

HEBREWS 6:18-19

Blessed are those who trust in the LORD and have made the LORD their hope and confidence.

JEREMIAH 17:7

The LORD says, . . . "I will fight those who fight you, and I will save your children."

ISAIAH 49:25

Peter replied, "Repent and be baptized, every one of you, in the name of Jesus Christ for the forgiveness of your sins. And you will receive the gift of the Holy Spirit. The promise is for you and your children and for all who are far off—for all whom the Lord our God will call."

ACTS 2:38-39, NIV

When [Christ] was hung on the cross, he took upon himself the curse for our wrongdoing. . . . Through Christ Jesus, God has blessed the Gentiles with the same blessing he promised to Abraham, so that we who are believers might receive the promised Holy Spirit through faith.

GALATIANS 3:13-14

I tell you, you can
pray for anything,
and if you believe
that you've received it,
it will be yours.

MARK 11:24

With God
everything is possible.

MATTHEW 19:26

"The message is very close at hand; it is on your lips and in your heart." And that message is the very message about faith that we preach: If you openly declare that Jesus is Lord and believe in your heart that God raised him from the dead, you will be saved.

ROMANS 10:8-9

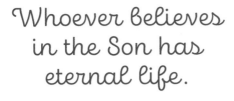

Whoever believes
in the Son has
eternal life.

JOHN 3:36, NIV

If the Son sets you free,
you are truly free.

JOHN 8:36

Because we are his children, God has sent
the Spirit of his Son into our hearts,
prompting us to call out, "Abba, Father."
Now you are no longer a slave but God's
own child. And since you are his child,
God has made you his heir.

GALATIANS 4:6-7

The Father who knows all hearts knows what the Spirit is saying, for the Spirit pleads for us believers in harmony with God's own will. And we know that God causes everything to work together for the good of those who love God and are called according to his purpose for them.

ROMANS 8:27-28

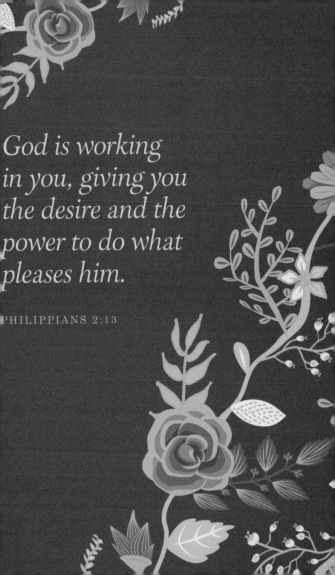

God is working
in you, giving you
the desire and the
power to do what
pleases him.

PHILIPPIANS 2:13

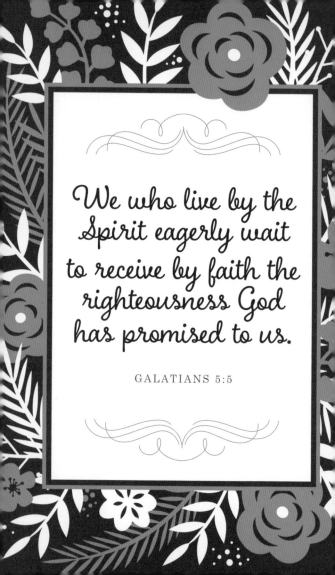

We who live by the Spirit eagerly wait to receive by faith the righteousness God has promised to us.

GALATIANS 5:5

I pray that God, the source of hope, will fill
you completely with joy and peace because
you trust in him. Then you will overflow
with confident hope through the power of
the Holy Spirit.

ROMANS 15:13

Thanks be to God! He gives us the victory through our Lord Jesus Christ. Therefore, my dear brothers and sisters, stand firm. Let nothing move you. Always give yourselves fully to the work of the Lord, because you know that your labor in the Lord is not in vain.

1 CORINTHIANS 15:57-58, NIV

God has said, "I will never fail you. I will never abandon you."

HEBREWS 13:5

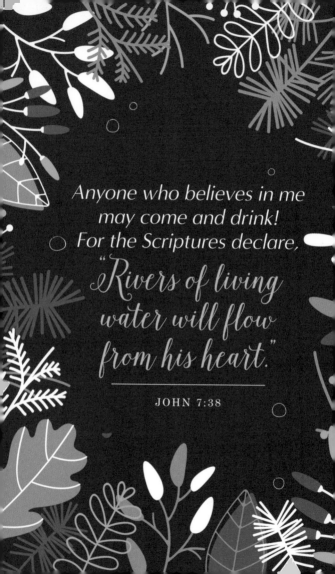

Anyone who believes in me
may come and drink!
For the Scriptures declare,
*"Rivers of living
water will flow
from his heart."*

JOHN 7:38

When the poor and needy search for water and there is none, and their tongues are parched from thirst, then I, the LORD, will answer them. I, the God of Israel, will never abandon them. I will open up rivers for them on the high plateaus. I will give them fountains of water in the valleys. I will fill the desert with pools of water.

ISAIAH 41:17-18

Jesus replied, "Anyone who drinks this water will soon become thirsty again. But those who drink the water I give will never be thirsty again. It becomes a fresh, bubbling spring within them, giving them eternal life."

JOHN 4:13-14

Fear the LORD,
you his godly people,
for those who fear
him will have all
they need.

PSALM 34:9

If you fully obey the
LORD your God . . .
*wherever you go and
whatever you do,
you will be blessed.*

DEUTERONOMY 28:1, 6

Christ himself gave the apostles, the prophets, the evangelists, the pastors and teachers, to equip his people for works of service, so that the body of Christ may be built up until we all reach unity in the faith and in the knowledge of the Son of God and become mature, attaining to the whole measure of the fullness of Christ.

EPHESIANS 4:11-13, NIV

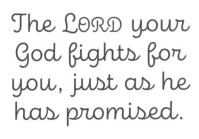

The LORD your
God fights for
you, just as he
has promised.

JOSHUA 23:10

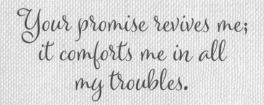

Your promise revives me;
it comforts me in all
my troubles.

PSALM 119:50

Can anything ever separate us from Christ's love? Does it mean he no longer loves us if we have trouble or calamity, or are persecuted, or hungry, or destitute, or in danger, or threatened with death? . . . No, despite all these things, overwhelming victory is ours through Christ, who loved us.

ROMANS 8:35, 37

This is real love—not that we loved God, but that he loved us and sent his Son as a sacrifice to take away our sins. Dear friends, since God loved us that much, we surely ought to love each other. No one has ever seen God. But if we love each other, God lives in us, and his love is brought to full expression in us.

1 JOHN 4:10-12

There is no fear
in love, but perfect
love casts out fear.

1 JOHN 4:18, ESV

Your promises have
been thoroughly
tested; that is why
I love them so much.

PSALM 119:140

God is not unjust. He will not forget how hard you have worked for him and how you have shown your love to him by caring for other believers, as you still do. Our great desire is that you will keep on loving others as long as life lasts, in order to make certain that what you hope for will come true.

HEBREWS 6:10-11

All who are victorious will be clothed
in white. I will never erase their names
from the Book of Life, but I will announce
before my Father and his angels that
they are mine.

REVELATION 3:5

The wages of sin is death; but the gift of God is eternal life through Jesus Christ our Lord.

ROMANS 6:23, KJV

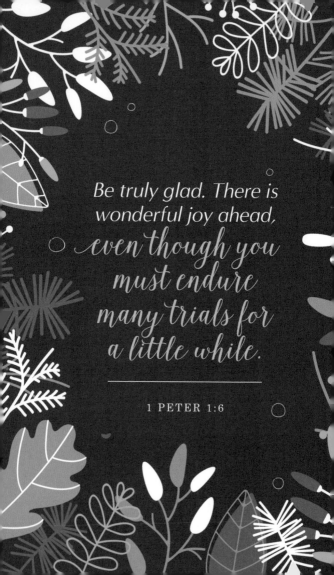

Be truly glad. There is wonderful joy ahead, *even though you must endure many trials for a little while.*

1 PETER 1:6

These trials will show that your faith is genuine. It is being tested as fire tests and purifies gold—though your faith is far more precious than mere gold. So when your faith remains strong through many trials, it will bring you much praise and glory and honor on the day when Jesus Christ is revealed to the whole world.

1 PETER 1:7

Our earthly fathers disciplined us for a few years, doing the best they knew how. But God's discipline is always good for us, so that we might share in his holiness. No discipline is enjoyable while it is happening—it's painful! But afterward there will be a peaceful harvest of right living for those who are trained in this way.

HEBREWS 12:10-11

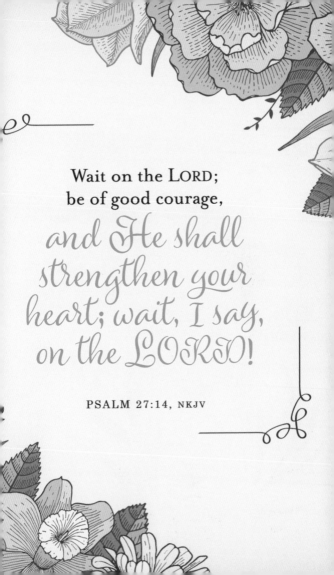

Wait on the LORD;
be of good courage,
and He shall
strengthen your
heart; wait, I say,
on the LORD!

PSALM 27:14, NKJV

I will be glad and rejoice
in your unfailing love,
*for you have seen
my troubles, and
you care about the
anguish of my soul.*

PSALM 31:7

Is anyone among you sick? Let him call for the elders of the church, and let them pray over him, anointing him with oil in the name of the Lord. And the prayer of faith will save the sick, and the Lord will raise him up. And if he has committed sins, he will be forgiven.

JAMES 5:14-15, NKJV

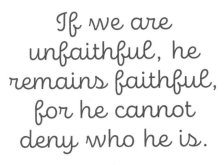

If we are unfaithful, he remains faithful, for he cannot deny who he is.

2 TIMOTHY 2:13

*If you forgive those
who sin against you,
your heavenly Father
will forgive you.*

MATTHEW 6:14

Don't repay evil for evil. Don't retaliate with insults when people insult you. Instead, pay them back with a blessing. That is what God has called you to do, and he will grant you his blessing.

1 PETER 3:9

Do not be anxious about anything, but in everything by prayer and supplication with thanksgiving let your requests be made known to God. And the peace of God, which surpasses all understanding, will guard your hearts and your minds in Christ Jesus.

PHILIPPIANS 4:6-7, ESV

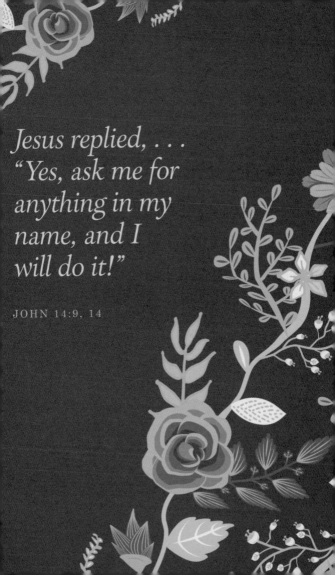

Jesus replied, . . .
"Yes, ask me for
anything in my
name, and I
will do it!"

JOHN 14:9, 14

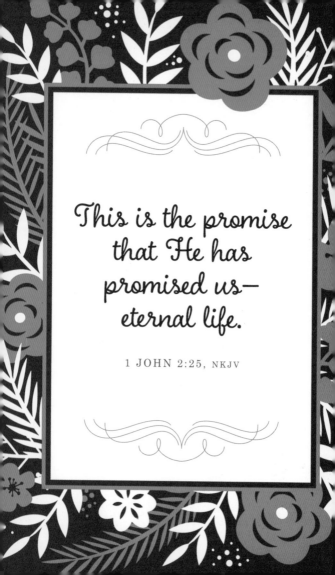

This is the promise
that He has
promised us—
eternal life.

1 JOHN 2:25, NKJV

We don't look at the troubles we can see now; rather, we fix our gaze on things that cannot be seen. For the things we see now will soon be gone, but the things we cannot see will last forever. For we know that when this earthly tent we live in is taken down (that is, when we die and leave this earthly body), we will have a house in heaven.

2 CORINTHIANS 4:18–5:1

By his divine power, God has given us
everything we need for living a godly life.
We have received all of this by coming to
know him, the one who called us to himself
by means of his marvelous glory and
excellence.

2 PETER 1:3

Let the Holy Spirit
guide your lives.
Then you won't
be doing what your
sinful nature craves.

GALATIANS 5:16

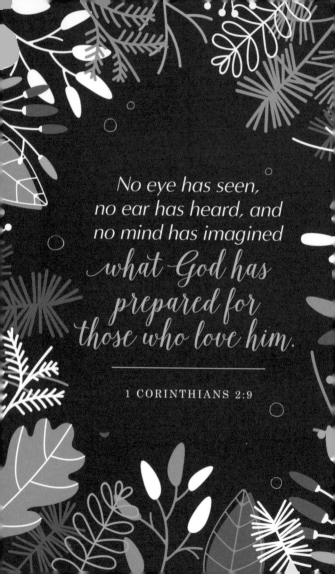

No eye has seen,
no ear has heard, and
no mind has imagined
what God has
prepared for
those who love him.

1 CORINTHIANS 2:9

We have a priceless inheritance—an inheritance that is kept in heaven for you, pure and undefiled, beyond the reach of change and decay. And through your faith, God is protecting you by his power until you receive this salvation, which is ready to be revealed on the last day for all to see.

1 PETER 1:4-5

We are always confident, knowing that while we are at home in the body we are absent from the Lord. For we walk by faith, not by sight. We are confident, yes, well pleased rather to be absent from the body and to be present with the Lord.

2 CORINTHIANS 5:6-8, NKJV

Let us hold tightly without wavering to the hope we affirm,

for God can be trusted to keep his promise.

HEBREWS 10:23

Jesus told them, . . .

"Heaven and earth
will disappear,
but my words will
never disappear."

MATTHEW 24:4, 35

Christ lives within you, so even though your body will die because of sin, the Spirit gives you life because you have been made right with God. The Spirit of God, who raised Jesus from the dead, lives in you. And just as God raised Christ Jesus from the dead, he will give life to your mortal bodies by this same Spirit living within you.

ROMANS 8:10-11

You will not leave my
soul among the dead
or allow your holy one
to rot in the grave.

PSALM 16:10

The trumpet will sound,
and the dead will be
raised imperishable, and
we shall be changed.

1 CORINTHIANS 15:52, ESV

We believers also groan, even though we have the Holy Spirit within us as a foretaste of future glory, for we long for our bodies to be released from sin and suffering. We, too, wait with eager hope for the day when God will give us our full rights as his adopted children, including the new bodies he has promised us.

ROMANS 8:23

The LORD of Heaven's Armies says, "The day of judgment is coming, burning like a furnace. On that day the arrogant and the wicked will be burned up like straw. They will be consumed—roots, branches, and all. But for you who fear my name, the Sun of Righteousness will rise with healing in his wings. And you will go free, leaping with joy like calves let out to pasture."

MALACHI 4:1-2

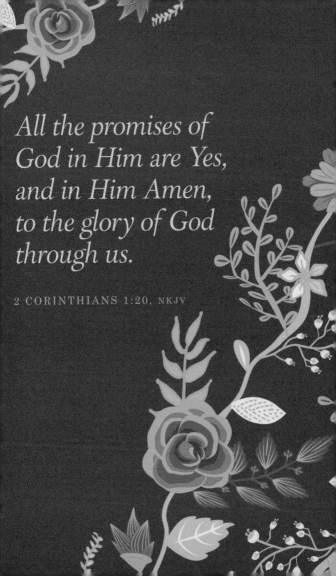

All the promises of God in Him are Yes, and in Him Amen, to the glory of God through us.

2 CORINTHIANS 1:20, NKJV

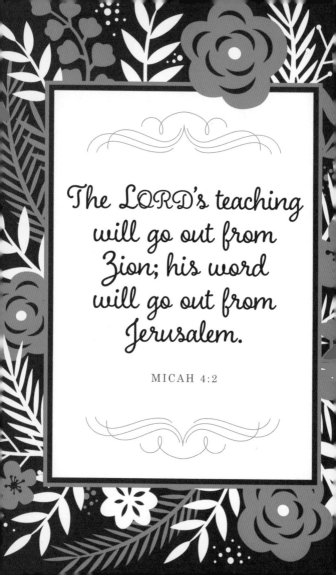

The LORD's teaching will go out from Zion; his word will go out from Jerusalem.

MICAH 4:2

In the last days, the mountain of the LORD's house will be the highest of all—the most important place on earth. . . . People from all over the world will stream there to worship. People from many nations will come and say, "Come, let us go up to the mountain of the LORD, to the house of Jacob's God. There he will teach us his ways, and we will walk in his paths."

ISAIAH 2:2-3

"In that coming day," says the LORD, "I will gather together those who are lame, those who have been exiles. . . . Those who are weak will survive as a remnant; those who were exiles will become a strong nation. Then I, the LORD, will rule from Jerusalem as their king forever."

MICAH 4:6-7

The LORD will be
king over all the earth.
On that day there will
be one LORD.

ZECHARIAH 14:9

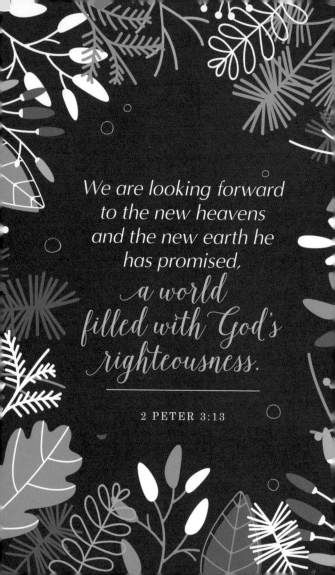

We are looking forward to the new heavens and the new earth he has promised, *a world filled with God's righteousness.*

2 PETER 3:13